SALT LAKE 2002

AN OFFICIAL BOOK OF THE OLYMPIC WINTER GAMES

Text by Lee Benson and Susan Easton Black

Photographs by John Telford

SHADOW MOUNTAIN

Visit us at www.shadowmountain.com

Library of Congress Cataloging-in-Publication Data

   Salt Lake 2002: an official book of the Olympic Winter
Games / Lee Benson, Susan Easton Black, and John Telford.
      p. cm.
ISBN 1-57345-795-7
   1. Winter Olympic Games (19th: 2002: Salt Lake City,
Utah)--Planning. I. Benson, Lee. II. Black, Susan Easton. III.
Telford, John. IV. Title.

GV842 2002.B52 2000
796.98--dc21   00-038747

Printed in the United States of America

10 9 8 7 6 5 4 3 2 1   42316-6628

Contents | Salt Lake 2002

ROCKY ANDERSON
SALT LAKE CITY MAYOR

As Salt Lake City prepares to host the 2002 Olympic and Paralympic Winter Games, we look forward to welcoming our friends from throughout the world. Our guests will discover a dynamic city with a pioneering spirit, an industrious people, and a quality of life unsurpassed in this country. As reflected recently in the Places Rated Almanac, Salt Lake City is the "Number One Place to Live" in America today.

All of our Olympic visitors—athletes and spectators alike—will find a city alive with celebration, excitement, and goodwill. Our diverse population is one of the most literate and multilingual anywhere, and our community is delighted at the prospect of hosting visitors from throughout the world for twenty-seven exhilarating days.

Our venue facilities and our Wasatch Mountain backdrop will establish new Olympic standards. More importantly, the pioneering, volunteer spirit of Utah's people will set new standards for Olympic warmth and welcoming.

The arrival of the 2002 Olympic and Paralympic Winter Games is a fulfillment of decades of hope and dedication on the part of many Utahns. We eagerly await the celebration and the challenge of making true the words "The World Is Welcome Here."

—Mayor Rocky Anderson

MICHAEL O. LEAVITT
GOVERNOR OF UTAH

The Salt Lake Winter Olympic Games promise the spirit and optimism of the American West, a celebration of athletes, and a passion for the land. The state of Utah is making a contribution of lasting value to the Olympic movement: not just a Games that is higher, faster, stronger, but an entire movement that is truer, nobler, and worthier. We look forward to welcoming the world in 2002.

—*Governor Michael O. Leavitt*

MITT ROMNEY
PRESIDENT, SALT LAKE ORGANIZING COMMITTEE FOR
THE OLYMPIC WINTER GAMES OF 2002

On behalf of the Olympic movement, let me say how proud we are to be welcoming the world to Salt Lake City in 2002. The Olympic Games are perhaps the most effective platform for celebrating character on the world stage. We will play host to young men and women from all around the globe, real heroes in many instances, who have overcome tremendous difficulties to push the boundaries of the physical body and of the human spirit. We will witness Olympic moments that will inspire us and will live in the imagination of our children. We will celebrate hard work, integrity, sacrifice and determination.

And Utah is the perfect setting for such drama. The scenery itself is dramatic. The snow and ice are among the best in the world. The people are warm-hearted and generous. And the spirit of pioneerism and all-encompassing commitment that are a part of the history and character of this place will resonate for all the world to see.

Bring on the games.

—W. Mitt Romney

SALT LAKE 2002

SALT LAKE CITY SKYLINE WITH
WASATCH MOUNTAINS AT DUSK

Chapter One | **The Quest**

IMBEDDED PROMINENTLY in the courtyard of a plaza in the heart of downtown Salt Lake City lie several dozen bricks engraved with the names of those who took the lead in winning the city's bid for the 2002 Olympic Winter Games.

Less than three years after the bricks were ceremoniously cemented in place, and with the 2002 Games still a distant four years away, fewer than six of the names memorialized were still associated with the committee organizing the Salt Lake Games.

Mute testimony of a scandal.

Not all of the organizational atrophy occurred because of the fallout of what would become known

around the world as the "Salt Lake bid scandal."
Many of those who had helped in Salt Lake's
successful bid to gain the Games simply moved on
to other pursuits, the unpaid volunteers to "real
jobs" and the civic supporters to other community
quests to champion. But there were others who did
not leave the Olympic stage of their own accord.
They were washed overboard by the backlash of a
wave of their own making.

The very zeal that so successfully brought the
Games to town in the first place, that scored an
unprecedented first-round knockout at the IOC voting in Budapest in 1995, that caused those engraved
bricks to be carefully placed in honor in the ground,
came back to take the bidders down with a
vengeance.

The good reputation of a city soon followed.

IT BEGAN WHEN an eighty-year-old Swiss gentleman cleared his throat and said aloud the word *bribe*.

It wasn't just any Swiss gentleman. It was Marc
Hodler, a member in good standing of the
International Olympic Committee (IOC) and the
head of the coordination commission overseeing the

SALT LAKE CITY AND COUNTY
BUILDING THROUGH WINDOWS OF
SCOTT M. MATHESON COURTHOUSE

*Looking for historic buildings? The City and County
Building and the Utah State Capitol are fine
examples of historic architecture. But don't miss the
Cathedral of St. Mark; built in 1871, it is the third-
oldest Episcopal church building in the United
States. It is unique, as is the Catholic Cathedral of
the Madeleine, a Gothic-styled masterpiece. These
beautiful cathedrals and government buildings have
been restored to their original splendor.*

organization of the Salt Lake 2002 Games. Standing inside the foyer of the IOC world headquarters building in Lausanne, Switzerland, Hodler responded to questions about reports that Salt Lake City's bid for the 2002 Games had allegedly involved favors for certain IOC delegates—favors that included college scholarships and employment for relatives as well as other assorted gifts, services and donations.

A veteran observer of many bid city campaigns and knowledgeable about the inner workings of the usually very private IOC, the soft-spoken Hodler, who had already been given a list by Salt Lake's bidders that detailed the incentives they had offered to some of his colleagues in the race for 2002, said bluntly of those incentives, "It's not wrong to say it's a bribe. It's a bribe.

"I'm terribly sorry that Salt Lake City, as by far the best place to hold the Olympic Winter Games, had to use certain methods to get the vote," Hodler went on. "That's too bad. If there's a city in the world that didn't need that, it was Salt Lake."

The date was 10 December 1998. By early the next morning, Hodler's words had circled the world. Within weeks, no fewer than four investigations had been ordered, one by the IOC itself, one by the

TRIAD CENTER AND DOWNTOWN HOTELS

In employment and income growth Utah consistently outpaces the national economy. Utah is known worldwide as a progressive, high-tech business state. Businesses like NuSkin, Aminco International, EK Ekcessories, Marker, O.C. Tanner, and Huntsman Chemical call Utah home.

United States Olympic Committee (USOC), one by the Salt Lake Organizing Committee (SLOC) and one by the United States Justice Department.

In the high-stakes playing fields of world-class extortion and underhanded bribery and deal making, Salt Lake's wining and dining of IOC delegates might have been strictly small time—it would soon be determined that barely more than a million dollars, total, was involved in Salt Lake's excessive courting of the IOC over a four-year period. But this, after all, was the Olympic Winter Games, bastion of the gods, domain of the noble warrior. If the Games weren't clean, what was?

IN SALT LAKE CITY, the center of the maelstrom, the court of public opinion rendered its verdict swift and harsh. Well before the formal investigations even began, let alone finished, the head-rolling commenced. The top two positions of the organizing committee were quickly vacated, with others soon to follow.

For a community that prided itself on honor, integrity and fair play, a place where some people still leave their doors unlocked at night, the mere suggestion that there might have been improper

courting—legal or not—was enough to lower the boom.

Later the evidence began pouring in: 13 college scholarships given, including 6 to relatives of IOC delegates. Expense-paid trips for IOC delegates and their entourages to ski resorts and Super Bowls. Free medical aid, complimentary airfare, lavish shopping sprees, specially arranged employment for IOC friends and family. There was even evidence of contributions to political campaigns and other causes close to the hearts of certain IOC delegates.

To many, there was no question that the bidders had pushed the business of securing IOC votes to the borders of good taste and beyond. As a result of Salt Lake's largesse, 10 members of the IOC would be expelled and another 10 sanctioned—the first expulsions and sanctions for corruption in the august body's century-plus existence. Strict rules for future bids were adopted, including the end of personal visits to bidding cities by the general IOC membership and careful enforcement of ceilings on acceptable gift giving. In addition, new term and age limits were applied to IOC membership, and, in an effort to bring sport back to the forefront, 15 former Olympic athletes were added to the committee.

BLACK ROCK, GREAT SALT LAKE

The Great Salt Lake, 70 miles long by 30 miles wide, is the largest American lake west of the Mississippi. Because it has no outlet, it is eight times saltier than the ocean, with a salt content as high as 27 percent. The density of the water virtually guarantees that bathers will float! The lake provides important wildlife resources as well as recreational opportunities.

MEANWHILE, IN SALT LAKE, Mitt Romney, a Massachusetts resident with Utah ties but no connections to the earlier bid committee, was brought in to lead the organizing committee, where the house-cleaning continued as several key members of the board of trustees stepped down because of potential conflicts of interest.

Knowing nothing more of the bid history or the scandal's details than what he'd read in the newspapers and seen on TV, Romney took the tack from the start to look forward, not behind. There were sponsors to re-enthuse and a budget to salvage—a budget suddenly $379 million in shortfall. Scandals do take their toll.

In reality, of course, bidding for the Games has historically been about adroit and clever maneuvering, if not outright quid pro quo. History is full of "creative" bid city lobbying. In the wake of the Salt Lake bid scandal, such a history would be revealed in more detail than ever before.

Unearthed by a worldwide media fact-digging frenzy, evidence of excessive gift giving and favor bestowing would be found in the bids of other recent qualifiers, including Atlanta, Nagano (whose bid documents were burned following the Olympic

BONNEVILLE SALT FLATS

Speed skating and downhill racing are fast! But if you want really fast—scary fast—try the Bonneville Salt Flats, about 90 miles west of Salt Lake City. In 1925 Ab Jenkins, driving an old Studebaker, raced an excursion train for two hundred miles across the salt beds. Jenkins beat the train by a margin of ten minutes. Ever since then, speed car racers have been breaking world land speed records on the salt flats.

Winter Games of 1998) and Sydney, as well as throughout the ranks of the IOC, reaching all the way to its upper tiers.

Salt Lake clearly wasn't the first city to play this game; it *was* the first city to have its tactics unravel so publicly. But whereas other cities might have used such history to defend their actions while exhaustively looking for a context that would ease their sting, Salt Lake chose to get out the whip and administer its own lashes—quickly, fervently and publicly. In the end, that seemed to say as much about the city as it did about its scandal.

PERHAPS THE BIGGEST LAMENT by those familiar with Salt Lake's position in the race for 2002—both from within the IOC and from neutral observers who understood the competition—was how unnecessary it was to oversell the bid. From the start, Salt Lake City was the 2002 front-runner. It lost out to Nagano for the right to host the 1998 Olympic Winter Games by only four votes, 46 to 42, in balloting that went to the wire at the 1991 IOC session in Birmingham, England. There were many who felt that if another U.S. city, Atlanta, hadn't surprisingly won

UTAH LAKE WITH WASATCH
MOUNTAINS IN BACKGROUND

It is recorded that Father Escalante and his party camped on the shores of Utah Lake more than 200 years ago. This freshwater lake, about 40 miles south of Salt Lake City, feeds into the Great Salt Lake via the Jordan River.

the rights for the 1996 Summer Games in an IOC vote held less than a year earlier, Salt Lake would have easily outdistanced Nagano for the 1998 bid.

Of the other contenders in Birmingham, only Salt Lake and Ostersund, Sweden, elected to stay the course and try again for 2002, giving Salt Lake the natural position as the city to beat. When a pair of newcomers, Quebec City, Canada, and Sion, Switzerland, later qualified to fill out the final 2002 ballot, it was no secret that they had plenty of ground to make up.

Salt Lake already had a thirty-year head start.

Utah's capital city first began lobbying for a spot in the Olympic Winter Games rotation in 1965, with an eye on winning the right to host the 1972 Games. Armed with a $35,000 budget and the blessings of the United States Olympic Committee, a delegation headed by Utah governor Calvin Rampton that carried the internationally savvy monogram of OUI—Olympics for Utah, Inc.—flew to Rome in the spring of 1966 and made what amounted to a half-day presentation to the IOC. The Utah delegates knew no one in the room. Sapporo, Japan, won that 1972 bid, outpolling Banff, Canada; Lahti, Finland; and Salt Lake City.

EVENING LIGHT ON TWIN PEAKS, MOUTH OF LITTLE COTTONWOOD CANYON

SALT LAKE VALLEY FROM
HIGH ON MOUNT OLYMPUS

Defeat notwithstanding, the Rome experience identified Salt Lake and its mountains as a bid hopeful—a new and upcoming, if slightly naïve, player in the field of international winter sports.

Less than two years later, after voters in Denver, Colorado, did a U-turn and elected to give back the bid their city had won for the 1976 Olympic Winter Games, Salt Lake—which had lost out to Denver in the American preliminaries for the 1976 bidding— was again in the mix, this time offering to step in and keep the Games in the Rocky Mountains, if just around the corner and on the other side of the Continental Divide. The IOC voted instead to return the 1976 Games to Innsbruck, Austria, where they had staged a successful run just 12 years earlier and where proven facilities were still in place. But, again, Salt Lake's hat was in the ring, its name recognition on the rise internationally.

In the 1980s, Salt Lake was back again, lobbying the USOC for another chance as America's choice. But the USOC picked Anchorage, Alaska. After Anchorage failed to make the cut in international bidding for the 1992 and 1994 Olympic Winter Games, however (they went to Albertville, France, and Lillehammer, Norway, respectively), the

SETTING MOON OVER HEBER
VALLEY, NEAR SOLDIER HOLLOW

USOC turned again to Salt Lake, this time with a conditional request.

Build the facilities first.

Tired of coming up short, and realizing that the international bidding game was becoming increasingly competitive, the USOC reasoned that the American city with the best chance would be the American city that was best prepared. That meant entering the race with ski jumps and hockey rinks and luge runs instead of promises.

Salt Lake had the mountains, it had the snowfall, and it certainly had the experience. Counting the times it lost out in the U.S. preliminaries to Anchorage, it had already been in the running four times, for the 1972, 1976, 1992 and 1994 Olympic Winter Games. It was time to fill the Wasatch Front with completed venues and then sit back and wait for someone to deliver the Olympic Flame.

The move was a gamble. Building ski jumps and ice sheets and bobsled tracks represented considerable seed money with no guarantee of return. But backed by a $59 million sales tax referendum approved by Utah voters, construction of the facilities began in early 1991—long before anyone knew when, or if, the "Build it and they will come" strategy would pay off.

TIMPOONEKE PEAK, NORTHERNMOST
PEAK OF MOUNT TIMPANOGOS

The first snows present a tranquil scene, but ardent hikers know it won't be long before harsh winds will strip leaves from the trees and rattle branches. If they want to reach the top of the rocky crags and an unequaled wilderness before winter's harsh storms, they must hurry. The snow on Utah's mountains, which are carved by ancient glaciers and sculpted by wind and water, does not wait for the last hiker. Only a few climbers reach their reward—solitude!

The first test came soon enough. Mere weeks after construction crews broke ground on the bob-sled and luge runs in the mountains east of Salt Lake, the IOC convened in Birmingham to decide the host city for the Olympic Winter Games of 1998. Among the contending cities that flew to England to make their presentations, Salt Lake City—which had pre-vailed over Anchorage, Lake Placid and Reno-Tahoe to become the USOC's representative—was hands down the best-preparing city in the field.

It still wasn't enough to avert defeat yet again—and to yet another entrant from Japan—as Salt Lake's lifetime bidding record for the Olympic Winter Games stretched to zero-for-five.

The post-Birmingham frustration was palpable, casting a pall over a bid team and a city that seem-ingly had it all—except the Games. Indeed, later on, after the "Bribegate" scandal exposed a Salt Lake zealousness for the 2002 bid far overshadowing any-thing in its bidding past, many would point to that frustration as the root cause. If having a Games-ready city wasn't enough, if being prepared and vir-tually ready to go wasn't going to cut it . . . then try another approach.

Still, by the time the vote for the 2002 Olympic

NEWFALLEN SNOW AT JORDAN
PINES, BIG COTTONWOOD CANYON

Some of the greatest ski runs in Utah are not slated as Olympic sites in 2002. In Big Cottonwood Canyon, the Solitude and Brighton ski resorts are popular destinations for tourists and local ski enthusiasts. Alta and Snowbird offer additional world-famous powder in neighboring Little Cottonwood Canyon.

Winter Games came along in Budapest in June
1995, no one doubted the depth of Salt Lake's pres-
ence on merit alone. Facilities that had been under
construction four years earlier were now completed.
The city that had been best prepared four years
before was even better prepared. And by now, in
sharp contrast to the Rome experience some 30
years before, the Salt Lake delegation not only knew
every delegate in the room but could recite what
each liked for breakfast.

To no one's surprise, Salt Lake won, although
the landslide by which it prevailed was a bit unex-
pected. The perennial bridesmaid belied its past by
capturing the bid on the very first ballot. Salt Lake
got 54 votes, Ostersund and Sion 14 apiece, and
Quebec 7. The outright majority was enough to elim-
inate the need for any further rounds of balloting,
since all nonmajority cities were eliminated. In more
than 70 years of IOC voting for Olympic Winter
Games sites, such a thing had never happened before.

Even without the nearly unanimous support it
got from IOC delegates representing African and
South American countries (votes that would come
under the spotlight in the later bribes-for-votes
scandal investigations), the overall voting support

GAMBLE OAK ARCHWAY, RED BUTTE
GARDENS, UNIVERSITY OF UTAH

indicated that Salt Lake would have still been in a dominant, seemingly unreachable position, the run-away choice for 2002 no matter what.

Whatever the case, the resounding Budapest vote ended three decades of frustration, and Salt Lake was ready for that end. Moments after the announcement, at an elegant reception center in Budapest, hundreds of Utah's most influential leaders, statesmen and supporters assembled to toast the sweet taste of victory, accept a congratulatory phone call from U.S. president Bill Clinton, and party long into the Hungarian night.

Meanwhile, back in Salt Lake, as soon as the good news was delivered, a crowd of more than 50,000 that had gathered on the grounds of the City and County Building literally began dancing in the street. State Street, to be exact. Salt Lake City was an Olympic city! Finally!

ENJOYING A NIGHT RIDE ON
SALT LAKE CITY'S MAIN STREET

HUNT PANEL, NINE-MILE CANYON,
FREMONT INDIAN PETROGLYPH

GREEN RIVER OVERLOOK,
CANYONLANDS NATIONAL PARK

STORM MOUNTAIN AREA,
BIG COTTONWOOD CANYON

Chapter Two | **The Place**

IT WAS LONG BEFORE the latter part of the 1900s, of course, that the facilities that would make Salt Lake City an attractive center for winter sport began to be put into place.

To get to the real beginning, go back 75 million years, to the Cretaceous Period of the earth's development, when the squeezing of the earth's surface began to push the land upward in what is now the western portion of North America. Other significant pushes would come along during the Eocene Epoch and, especially, the Pleistocene Epoch, a mere 2 million years ago. Mix in an Ice Age and millions of years of rain and wind and the result is the Rocky Mountains, at 3,000 miles the second-longest stretch of mountains on the planet (only the Andes are longer).

It is the Wasatch Range of the Middle Rockies that rises abruptly out of the east side of the Salt Lake Valley, more than 200 miles long, with peaks that reach almost to the 12,000-foot level from a valley floor some 7,500 feet below.

The contrast between the flat valley and the jutting mountains is dramatic and awe inspiring. And for the first people to permanently settle there, you could add "daunting" to the list of adjectives.

Legend has it that when the Mormon pioneers first laid eyes on the valley of the Great Salt Lake they saw exactly one tree—the same tree the Donner Party had seen the year before and hurried past in search of greener pastures. Legend further has it that when mountain man Jim Bridger, who knew every barren inch of the land, heard that the pioneers actually intended to stay, he offered a thousand dollars to anyone who could grow an ear of corn. *Hartford Times* editor Samuel Boyles said of the Salt Lake Valley, "It is a region whose uses are unimaginable, unless to hold the rest of the globe together."

In the summer of 1847, the future host city for

ANTELOPE ISLAND,
GREAT SALT LAKE

When John C. Fremont and Kit Carson had a successful antelope hunt on one of the large islands of the Great Salt Lake in 1845, they named the place Antelope Island in gratitude. It became a state park in 1993 and boasts bathing beaches, a sailboat marina, trails for hiking and biking, and areas for overnight camping. Antelope Island is also home to a herd of about 600 bison.

the Olympic Winter Games, lost deep in the Rocky Mountains, was one hundred percent potential.

The Indians and the fur trappers didn't want it. Neither did the gold diggers. For those early settlers looking for a place to call their own, that was the good news. It was also the bad news.

Horace Greeley, the *New York Tribune* newspaper editor of "Go West, Young Man" fame, made it clear he didn't mean *this* part of the West. "Let the Mormons have the territory to themselves," Greeley wrote. "It is worth very little to others."

In many ways, then, the unlikely rise of the host city for the 2002 Olympic Winter Games parallels that of an Olympian—right down to the Spartan beginnings and the quest to accomplish something in the face of incredibly long odds.

Indeed, if the athletes of 2002 find themselves seeking inspiration during the Games, they could do worse than look at the city at their feet. They might start at the site where the stump of that original lone tree still stands: at the corner of 300 South and 600 East near the heart of the city, about halfway between the Olympic Stadium and the Olympic Medals Plaza.

Then they could gaze around them at a valley filled with trees.

SNOW-COVERED PINES, CEDAR BREAKS
NATIONAL MONUMENT

TREES IN SNOW, THE SPRUCES,
BIG COTTONWOOD CANYON

The problem that original tree identified to all who saw it was that a valley bordered by the largest inland lake in western America was nonetheless in serious need of fresh water. Most took one look and moved on. The Mormon pioneers, on the other hand, took one look . . . and looked for a solution.

There was fresh water in the mountains, plenty of it. Maybe the huge lake that stretched to the west as far as the eye could see was worthless, with a concentration of salt many times that of the ocean. Maybe the annual rainfall in the valley was less than fifteen inches, making it officially a desert. But in the pine-covered mountains that surrounded the valley—the Wasatch Range to the east and the Oquirrh Range to the west—fresh water rolled in creeks and streams and flowed from springs.

It was this water supply that the early pioneer settlers diverted toward their crops of corn and potatoes and wheat, letting it gravitate downward through an intricate network of ditches. Thus was "modern irrigation" begun, and in the middle of nowhere and the midst of nothing, Salt Lake City was born.

More than a century and a half later, most of the irrigation ditches are gone, replaced by

BIG COTTONWOOD CREEK

Although the Salt Lake Valley was a desert when the Mormon pioneers arrived, water was plentiful in the nearby mountain streams. An ambitious irrigation system brought the water to the settlers' crops. Big Cottonwood Creek is still an important watershed for the area today.

concrete in one form or another. Skyscrapers here, highways there, housing developments and shopping malls beyond that, and finally, ice sheets and hockey stadiums.

The barren valley nobody wanted isn't so barren anymore. Its trees and fountains and ornate buildings and sparkling new arenas are a tribute to people who looked at what might be rather than what was. Times do change. The Salt Lake Valley's challenges now are the direct opposite of those encountered in 1847: so many people, so much growth, so much attention, so many more wanting to stay.

From the start, Salt Lake City has been a gathering place for the world. It was as if the greening of the valley acted as a kind of clarion call to the corners and cultures of the earth.

In that first group of permanent settlers that arrived in 1847, dozens of old-world European roots were already represented. In the decades since, virtually every culture in the world has found its way to the Salt Lake melting pot. It will be rare, if not impossible, for an Olympic visitor to arrive in February 2002 and not find some evidence of his or her homeland. In World Cup skiing events and other international sporting competitions held in advance

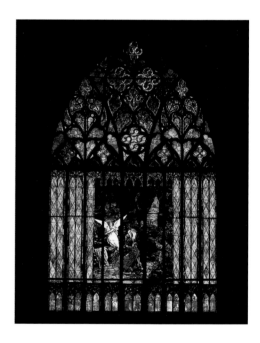

STAINED-GLASS WINDOW,
FIRST PRESBYTERIAN CHURCH,
SALT LAKE CITY

INTERIOR OF THE CATHEDRAL
OF THE MADELEINE, A CATHOLIC
CHURCH BUILDING ERECTED IN
THE LATE 1800S

Utah's religious mosaic is unexpectedly diverse. Members of more than 60 different religious denominations practice their faith in Utah, 12 with roots in the state that date back more than a hundred years. Just name a church, and you are likely to find it in Utah.

of the Olympic Winter Games, it has been common to see among the spectators cheering sections for the Swiss, the Norwegians, the Finns, the Germans, the Japanese, the Austrians, the Swedes and so forth— all of them made up of "native" Utahns whose roots and allegiances stretch far beyond the oceans.

Keeping connected to who you are and where you came from is in fact more of a favorite pastime in Salt Lake City than anywhere on earth. Each year, millions visit the world's largest genealogical library in downtown Salt Lake to search out their ancestors and identify their family pedigrees.

The genealogical library is just one of many landmarks of The Church of Jesus Christ of Latter-day Saints, also known as the "Mormons," to be found in the city. At the center is the Salt Lake Temple and surrounding Temple Square, from which the city's street grid system emanates. Examples of Mormon architecture and culture abound, including two intact houses of Mormon colonizer Brigham Young, located just a block from the temple. Members of the Mormon faith, many of them descendants of those original pioneers, make up roughly half of the city's modern population. The headquarters of the church that found a refuge in the

SALT LAKE TEMPLE AT
CHRISTMASTIME

Temple Square, in downtown Salt Lake City, is one of the premiere tourist attractions in Utah. "In no other city does a tourist out for a good time devote so much time to religion as in Salt Lake City," penned a reporter for the *St. Louis Star. More than 7 million visitors come to Temple Square each year to enjoy free guided tours, concert series, historical presentations, organ recitals, and rehearsals of the famous Mormon Tabernacle Choir. Others simply find peace strolling on sculptured walkways amid carefully placed Christmas lights or beautifully planned gardens.*

Rockies continues to occupy a prominent portion of the downtown area.

Perhaps the most noticeable contribution of the Mormon culture to the Olympic Winter Games will be the abundance of home-grown linguists. The Wasatch Front is full of returned Mormon missionaries who developed fluency in a wide variety of languages while living in foreign lands. Many of them will be at the assistance of the Salt Lake Organizing Committee throughout the course of the Games.

That kind of available man- and woman-power points to what may well emerge as the legacy of the Salt Lake Olympic Winter Games: a legacy of people as the most valuable resource of 2002. Although the mountains above Salt Lake City are large, tall and spectacular, they aren't as large, tall and spectacular as the Alps. And though the venues are solid and well built, many are not as exotic or artistic as those built by the Japanese, the Norwegians or others.

But in the state with the youngest average age in the United States as well as the highest birthrate, a place that has long attracted immigrants from around the globe, it is people that abound. People of all ages, backgrounds and abilities; energetic, service

MAURICE ABRAVANEL HALL,
HOME OF THE UTAH SYMPHONY

Excellence in the performing arts has become Salt Lake's signature. Whether performing Brahms' Symphony No. 3 or Handel's Messiah, the Utah Symphony never ceases to amaze audiences at Abravanel Hall in downtown Salt Lake. Likewise, sophisticated crowds are delighted with the performances of Ballet West. If a musical, operetta, classical play or evening of fine dining is more to your taste, Salt Lake offers a nightly smorgasbord to all in the "black tie" mood.

oriented, technologically savvy—and there's a good chance they speak your language.

The place that will host the 2002 Olympic Winter Games is many things to many people. It is a cultural capital, a religious capital, a business and technology capital, an education capital, a tourism capital, a medical capital, an entertainment capital, a sports capital and much, much more. All at the same time.

Its appeal is wide ranging. Some come for a glimpse of the world's largest open-pit copper mine, a vast hole that annually produces 15 percent of America's copper and is two and a half miles wide and as deep as the Grand Canyon. Others come to hear the 320-voice Mormon Tabernacle Choir sing "The Battle Hymn of the Republic" on the longest-running network radio program in America. Some do business with Novell or Iomega or Unisys or any of a number of cutting-edge technology industries. Many come to watch some of the best basketball played anywhere in the world: In the past decade alone, the Utah Jazz have played for the champion-ship of the National Basketball Association twice, and the University of Utah's men's team has

CART CREEK BRIDGE, FLAMING GORGE
NATIONAL RECREATION AREA

repeatedly contended for the national collegiate title, with an appearance in the national finals in 1998.

Others come to study and do research at the University of Utah, with its more than 90 graduate-level disciplines, or at the state's other institutions of higher learning. Some come for the services of the Huntsman Cancer Institute, one of the world's foremost cancer research and care facilities. Many come to attend the internationally acclaimed Sundance Film Festival, or to hear the internationally decorated Utah Symphony, or to ski and snowboard on the powder snow at any of the nearby and numerous world-class resorts. Or, if it's summer, many visitors will golf at the more than one hundred courses in the state—a higher percentage of golf courses, per capita, than anywhere else in the country.

Still others come for the wide open spaces beyond the Wasatch Front: to ride on the gravity-defying slickrock mountain bike trail in Moab; or to run the rapids of the Colorado River until it spills into the warm, bass-filled waters of Lake Powell; or to drive across the stark, level enormity of the Bonneville Salt Flats; or to visit one or all of the dozen national parks, monuments and

KAYAKING ON THE COLORADO
RIVER NEAR MOAB, UTAH

RIVER RAFTING CAMPSITE ON THE
GREEN RIVER, IN DINOSAUR
NATIONAL MONUMENT

recreation areas located from one tip of the state of Utah to the other.

In less than half a day's drive from Salt Lake City, it is possible to go to these parks and monuments and effectively leave all of civilization behind. This is especially true in the winter, when such southern outposts as Zion National Park, Arches National Park and Canyonlands National Park are largely devoid of their summer crowds but not their year-round geologic wonders or agreeable weather conditions.

These are places that need to be seen to be appreciated, places such as Monument Valley Navajo Tribal Park, an 8,000-acre preserve tucked within the spacious Navajo Reservation that straddles the Utah-Arizona border. Scattered throughout Monument Valley are massive red sandstone pillars of varying widths and heights, millions of years in the making, backdrop to numerous automobile commercials and even more Western movies. Once, when asked why Hollywood would go to all the trouble to lug cameras, cast and all the movie-making gear to the isolation of Monument Valley, John Wayne replied, "You have to do it where God put the West."

If it all sounds a bit paradoxical—wide open

WILD HORSE MESA, NEAR
GOBLIN VALLEY STATE PARK

DELICATE ARCH,
ARCHES NATIONAL PARK

———————

Want to see the rainbow-turned-to-stone? Delicate
Arch is just one formation in a geological
wonderland of arches, spires and Indian rock art
that awaits visitors in Utah's desert wilderness.
Visitors love to explore the more than 2,000 arches,
domes, cliffs, spires, buttes and mesas in colorful
southern Utah.

spaces interspersed with world gatherings of Olympic proportion—it's only because it is. Salt Lake City with its surroundings continues to be what it always has been: a work in progress, its future always hooking up with its past.

Nowhere is this symbolized more visually than at a spot immediately south of where the 2002 Olympic Village will house athletes and officials, just east of the city on the edge of the University of Utah campus. Nestled there in the foothills is an array of glass and steel buildings that make up the university's Research Park—a place where doctors, scientists, technicians and researchers are attempting to figure out how to, among other things, produce artificial limbs, cure blindness and, at the Huntsman Institute, come up with a cure for cancer.

No more than a long stone's throw away from all this cutting-edge research are This Is the Place Monument and adjoining Pioneer Trails State Park. It was from this vantage point in 1847 that Brigham Young, sick with fever, reputedly lifted his head up long enough to look out of the carriage in which he was traveling and stated, despite his weakened condition and the forlorn state of the valley below him, "This is the right place, drive on."

THIS IS THE PLACE MONUMENT,
SCULPTED BY MAHONRI YOUNG.

BAS-RELIEF PANEL AT BASE OF
THIS IS THE PLACE MONUMENT

In the pioneer village next to the monument, meticulous efforts have been made to re-create the conditions experienced by those early settlers. Visitors can walk the dirt streets, duck in and out of the log houses, corrals and shops, mingle with staff dressed in pioneer garb and be transported back to frontier times—as long as they don't let their eyes wander next door to Research Park or notice all those trees in the valley.

Even the most ardent and industrious of visitors to the 2002 Olympic Winter Games will be hard-pressed to capture all that the area and the surrounding state of Utah was, is, and is aspiring to become. At the start of a new millennium, it is a place where Indians ride their ponies in the southeast and where United States Air Force jet pilots fly their F-16s in the northwest. It is a place where cowboys drive cattle and computer aces push the borders of hard drives. It is a place of enormous emptiness and enormous growth. It is a place of Rocky Mountain isolation mere minutes from one of the busiest airports on earth.

A place now, as then, of unimaginable uses.

MOUNT POWELL, HENRY'S FORK
BASIN, HIGH UINTAH MOUNTAINS

The Uintah Mountains form the only mountain range in the United States that runs east and west. With their numerous lakes and streams and breathtaking scenery, they are a favorite destination of backpackers and fishermen.

LAKE POWELL FROM AHLSTROM POINT,
GLEN CANYON NATIONAL RECREATION AREA

DEEP POWDER SNOW, MOUNT
SUPERIOR, ALTA, UTAH

Chapter Three | The Games

WHEN THE MORMON PIONEERS, on their way from the eastern United States to settle in the uninhabited Great Salt Lake Valley, first cast their eyes on the enormous peaks in front of them, some must have wondered if they'd walked the wrong direction and run smack into the European Alps.

Familiarity would soon lead to compatibility, however, and as the settlement in Great Salt Lake City began to grow and prosper, the mountains that at first seemed to be a blockade became a life-giving resource, providing food, water, building materials, even protection.

And, finally, a little sport.

Snowfall in the Wasatch is both considerable and unique. Considerable because the high mountain peaks are the first formidable line of constraint for storms that start thousands of miles away in the Pacific Ocean and ride the jet stream eastward, picking up steam all the way. Unique because just before the storms slam into the Wasatch Range they pass over the Great Salt Lake, the biggest inland body of water in the western United States. While cruising thousands of feet above the lake's surface, the storms, like a fine French sauce, pick up just a pinch of salt. When the nearby mountains cash in the storm's deposit, the result is a brand of snow unlike that found anywhere else, lighter and fluffier. As the skiers came to call it: "powder." Or, as the state slogan on the Utah license plates proclaims it, "The Greatest Snow on Earth."

Scandinavian immigrants transplanted to the Wasatch were the first to play in the light mountain snow with relish. It reminded them of home and the sports they played there. Ski jumps began to pop up in the tops of the mountains as the 19th century made way for the 20th, and miners in the gold and silver boomtowns of Alta and Park City began making skis from wooden slats and sliding down the

HOARFROST ON COTTONWOOD
TREES, MOUNT TIMPANOGOS

The beauty and fragility of a winter scene are captured in myriads of snow crystals. Each crystal is unique in its shape and pattern, yet each has only six sides and contains less water than a raindrop. Although they are small and appear of no consequence, when piled high and deep, snow crystals create a snowpack on Utah's mountains that few areas can rival. It is no wonder that the snow crystal was selected as the Salt Lake 2002 Olympic emblem.

steep mountainsides after, and sometimes before, striking it rich.

As America dug itself out of the Great Depression in the 1930s and Utah's mining heyday simultaneously screeched to a halt, winter sports began to expand greatly along the Wasatch. The mines' demise was the mountaintop's rise. At Alta, the indomitable Alf Engen—a Norwegian immigrant who would emerge as the George Washington of western skiers—had the vision to turn the treeless ghost town into a skiing paradise that would boast the second chairlift in the country.

More mining towns past their time as well as other resorts would follow Alta's lead. In the early 1960s, Park City suspended all mining operations and turned its attention to the gold that could be mined above the ground. By the winter of 1963–64, when Park City opened its first season of skiing with the longest gondola (2.5 miles) in the world, the Wasatch Front was lined with ski resorts, from Beaver Mountain above Logan to Timphaven (now Sundance) above Provo, and all points in between.

Just a little over a year later, the first official committee was convened to investigate exactly how Salt Lake City, the capital and focal point of all this

HISTORIC DISTRICT,
PARK CITY, UTAH

Park City is an old silver-mining boomtown. Ski runs named Pick 'n' Shovel, Eureka, Claim Jumper and Prospector are reminders of the city's colorful past. Old western buildings now converted into restaurants, bars, clubs, shops, boutiques and art galleries are also reminders of gun-toting yesteryears. You'll enjoy the nightlife on Main Street, but you might also consider a hot-air balloon ride, a sleigh ride by moonlight or a slide down an old silver-mining shaft.

burgeoning winter sport, might go about qualifying
to become a host to the biggest winter sport festival
of them all: the Olympic Winter Games.

TO SAY THAT THE 2002 GAMES will be the
biggest Olympic Winter Games in history is not
hyperbole or subjective city pride. It is simply a
matter of fact. More athletes from more countries in
more sports than ever before will compete in front of
more spectators in the biggest city to ever host the
Olympic Winter Games.

   More than 2,600 athletes representing 80 countries will be in attendance—about 200 more athletes
and 8 more countries than attended the previous
Olympic Winter Games in Nagano, Japan, and a
fourth again bigger than the Lillehammer 1994
Games.

   In Salt Lake, athletes will compete in 15 disciplines and 78 medal events, up 10 events from
Nagano and more than double the 38 events held at
the last Olympic Winter Games in America—in Lake
Placid, New York, in 1980.

   For an Olympic Winter Games, the numbers
are huge. Huge enough that the television networks

MASS START, CROSS-COUNTRY
COMPETITION, SOLDIER HOLLOW

paid a record amount for the broadcast rights, including $545 million from NBC Television for the U.S. rights. They expect audiences worldwide in the 2 billion range—the most for any Games ever, winter or summer.

The numbers are first and foremost a tribute to the increasing popularity of the winter side of the Olympic Games, a side that didn't get rolling in its own right until almost thirty years after the first summer Games were held in Athens in 1896. Only the sport of figure skating, which was first contested as an Olympic event as part of the summer program in London in 1908, predated the first official Olympic Winter Games, held in 1924 in Chamonix, France. There, 16 countries and 294 athletes (including 13 women) participated in the Chamonix International Winter Sports Week, so called in an attempt to avoid conflict with purists who thought the Olympic Games should stay off the ice and the snow.

Only after the Chamonix Games were successfully concluded and a tidy profit was in the bank did the name change to include the Olympic designation. Thirteen medal events took place in Chamonix, a small French ski village not far from the Swiss border at the base of Mont Blanc, the highest peak in Europe.

FREESTYLE AERIAL SKIING,
DEER VALLEY

SNOWBOARDING, DEER VALLEY

The events included the four-man bobsled, men's ice hockey, men's and ladies' figure skating, pairs' figure skating, ski jumping, nordic combined, men's speed skating races at 500, 1,500, 5,000 and 10,000 meters, and men's cross-country races at 15 and 50 kilometers. Those 13 events will also be held in Salt Lake in 2002—along with 65 more.

Who could have guessed, walking the streets of Chamonix three-quarters of a century ago, that so many winter sports developments were just around the corner? Still to come were alpine skiing, luge racing, a skating technique for cross-country skiing, freestyle skiing, snowboarding, and dozens of other inventions and variations that would evolve from Chamonix's original theme. Now, as then, the basic premise of the Olympic Winter Games remains: For an event to qualify, it must be done on either snow or ice.

As the years have passed and the Olympic Winter Games have come and gone, each host city has made its mark, adding touches here, contributing innovations there, establishing individual identities, as winter sports have evolved, developed . . . and grown.

Seventy-eight years later, it is Salt Lake's fortune to inherit this developing winter legacy and add its

WOMEN'S SLALOM, OLYMPIC
TEST EVENT, DEER VALLEY

MEN'S DOWNHILL OLYMPIC
TEST EVENT, SNOWBASIN

own chapter and identity. The capital of the state of Utah will be the sixteenth city ever to host the Olympic Winter Games, placing it in rather an exclusive world fraternity. In all, 18 Olympic Winter Games have preceded Salt Lake, in ten countries, with three of the host cities holding two Games each. The complete lineup:

Chamonix, France, 1924

St. Moritz, Switzerland, 1928, 1948

Lake Placid, New York, USA, 1932, 1980

Garmisch-Partenkirchen, Germany, 1936

Oslo, Norway, 1952

Cortina, Italy, 1956

Squaw Valley, California, USA, 1960

Innsbruck, Austria, 1964, 1976

Grenoble, France, 1968

Sapporo, Japan, 1972

Sarajevo, Yugoslavia, 1984

Calgary, Canada, 1988

Albertville, France, 1992

Lillehammer, Norway, 1994

Nagano, Japan, 1998

Salt Lake City, Utah, USA, 2002

Each Olympic Winter Games has of course left its own indelible mark. Some are remembered for

innovations, such as St. Moritz, which introduced a separate alpine skiing program for the first time in 1948; or Squaw Valley, which opened the door for women speed skaters to perform on the Olympic stage. Some included unforgettable performances, such as the Grenoble Games, starring downhill skier Jean-Claude Killy, or the Games of Garmisch-Partenkirchen, where Sonja Henie cemented her figure skating legacy with her third straight gold medal. And still others offered the unusual and the extreme—who can forget Britain's Eddie "The Eagle" Edwards dropping like a stone off the ski jump in Calgary, or the 16 consecutive days of sunshine during the entire course of the Olympic Winter Games hosted in Lillehammer? While Salt Lake's niche in Olympic history is yet to be established, its program and projected innovations are already in place, giving some hint as to what to expect.

Of the 10 new events awaiting their debut in Salt Lake, perhaps the most attention-getting will be the skeleton—for two reasons. One, it is a dangerous event: Skeleton racers routinely reach speeds up to 70 miles per hour. Two, anyone who has ever ridden a sled or an inner tube down a hill can relate. The sport essentially involves lying face down on a

SKI-JUMPING COMPETITORS

YOUNG OLYMPIC HOPEFUL TAKES
THE SKI JUMP AT THE UTAH
WINTER SPORTS PARK

To be competitive on an international level, ski
jumpers start at a very early age. The competitors
shown here began jumping at age five. Now, five years
later, they are soaring the length of a football field.

souped-up, streamlined sled and riding it as fast as possible to the bottom of the hill. Strictly speaking, the skeleton is not a new event at all. It has been held twice before in the Olympic Winter Games, both times at St. Moritz (1928 and 1948) on the Cresta toboggan run at the St. Moritz resort. Because only St. Moritz has the unique Cresta run, no other Games cities scheduled the skeleton. But as the century wore on, skeleton enthusiasts began to fan out to traditional bobsled and luge tracks, where they found a new and ready place to compete. Both men and women will compete in the skeleton at the Utah Olympic Park just east of Salt Lake—the first Olympic site ever to host the event outside of St. Moritz.

Also at the Utah Olympic Park, the first-ever women's bobsleigh races will take place. Other new events in the 2002 lineup will include men's and women's biathlon pursuit races, cross-country sprint races for both men and women, a 1,500-meter short track speed skating race for both sexes, and a new sprint category in the nordic combined men's competition.

Apart from the expanded program, the record number of entrants, the record number of tickets available (exceeding 1.6 million) and the record

SHORT TRACK SPEED SKATING, THE PEAKS ICE ARENA, UTAH VALLEY

number of participating countries, what may well separate the Salt Lake 2002 Games from all that have preceded it is the sheer size and practicality of the place itself. In all its meanderings through the mountains of the world, most of the time in villages no more complex or demanding than the two-lane roads that serve them, never has the Olympic Movement seen anything like what it will see in and around Salt Lake.

The Wasatch Front's metropolitan population of 1.5 million people is enough to account for all the citizens of Chamonix, St. Moritz, Lake Placid, Garmisch-Partenkirchen, Cortina, Squaw Valley, Innsbruck, Grenoble, Sapporo, Albertville and Lillehammer combined—with people to spare. Only four times has the Olympic Winter Games stopped in cities of size—at Oslo, Sarajevo, Calgary and Nagano—and none of those cities approached the population, the scope or the relative compactness of the Wasatch Front. None was as close to its ski runs and jumps, nor as large at its center, nor as expansive in its suburbs. In sheer size and numbers, the Salt Lake 2002 Games will have the most hotel rooms (more than 35,000 within a two-hour radius of the city center), the largest airport (more than 21 million

SALT LAKE CITY, NESTLED IN THE
BEAUTIFUL WASATCH MOUNTAINS,
IS AN IDEAL OLYMPIC SITE

visitors a year), the widest roads and the most people living nearby in history.

Will that translate to an Olympic Winter Games as charming and aesthetically beautiful as those held in villages and cities far off the beaten path? Will the Salt Lake Games more resemble a summer Olympics? Will the Games be dwarfed by the landscape? Only time will tell.

On paper, the advantages are many. Traffic, much of it on freeways six lanes wide, should move freely, thanks largely to two major transportation improvement projects begun shortly after the city's Olympic bid was secured in 1995. One project involved a $1.35 billion remodel of the I-15 freeway that parallels the Wasatch Front. The other constructed a light-rail train line along roughly the same corridor.

Locals had to agree to put up with nearly three years of "road closed" signs and detours, with a promise of a freeway system as smooth and efficient as any in the country and a railway system that would take pressure off the freeways. That, and hassle-free driving for Olympic guests in 2002. As for the mountain areas serving the Salt Lake Games, all are accessible by freeways and major four-lane roads.

Flights in and out of an international airport

THE BANGERTER HIGHWAY INTERCHANGE IN THE SOUTH SALT LAKE VALLEY WELCOMES OLYMPIC VISITORS

that connects with all other major national hubs and is just minutes from the city center should also be more accessible than at any time in the past. Train and bus service, too, is direct to Salt Lake City, a city that has been known since its pioneer beginnings as the "Crossroads of the West."

Such convenience and services are expected to attract the largest crowds in Olympic Winter Games history. More people than ever before will have easy access to every event and every venue. Nothing in the Salt Lake Games will be remote or hard to get to. No events will be held in box canyons or at the end of dead-end roads. For the natives, that should mean smooth sailing and business as usual, without the wholesale road closures that have been necessary in other Olympic cities.

At those events that require no admission fees—the pin-trading center, for example, or the Olympic Medals Plaza near the city center, where nightly ceremonies will recognize each day's gold, silver and bronze medalists—crowds could and should exceed any ever seen in the history of the Games.

Another factor that is expected to contribute to record numbers of visitors and spectators is the normally agreeable weather of Salt Lake City and the

AUTUMN SNOWFALL,
LITTLE COTTONWOOD CANYON

WILDFLOWERS IN ALBION
BASIN BENEATH DEVIL'S CASTLE,
ALTA, UTAH

nearby mountains. Salt Lake sits in a temperate four-season zone. Winters are neither particularly long nor particularly cold, especially when compared to more extreme northern cities that have hosted the Olympic Winter Games in the past. In February, the month when the 2002 Games will be held, the average daytime city temperature is 37 degrees Fahrenheit (3 degrees Celsius), and the average daily snowfall is two inches. It will not be unusual if the Salt Lake 2002 Games feature some blue-sky, "shirtsleeve" days.

Such were the facts, figures and local details laid out by the Salt Lake bidders when they made their Olympic pitch—facts, figures and details that portend an Olympics of proportions never before seen.

Eighteen Olympic Winter Games ago, when the winter movement began with its original 13 events in Chamonix, perhaps Salt Lake City would have been too large and imposing to make a good fit. Certainly it was not prepared as a winter sports capital in 1924.

But the movement moves and grows, picking up steam with increasing numbers and interest. As the Olympic Winter Games begins a new century and a new millennium, all indications are that Salt Lake City will prove to be a perfect fit.

TORCH RUN AT
SOLITUDE SKI RESORT

On 18 March 1939, the first ski lift in Utah opened. Fifty excited Salt Lake businessmen attended the opening ceremony. A local reporter assigned to cover the event garnered only an inch of newsprint to hype the possibility of Utah's mountains attracting skiers. The inch was ignored, and the ski lift at Alta was a dismal failure the first season. But by the second season 86,000 skiers had purchased lift tickets. Today skiing is a $500 million annual industry in Utah.

MOUNT TIMPANOGOS

HISTORIC DEVEREAUX HOUSE WITH
SALT LAKE CITY IN BACKGROUND

Chapter Four | **The Venues**

J

JUST HOW COMPACT and accessible are these Games of Salt Lake? Consider this: It would be possible to click into your skis at the start gate of the Olympic downhill course at the top of the Snowbasin Ski Resort on Mount Ogden, take off down the hill, jump into your car, and be at the other extreme end of the Olympic corridor, the women's hockey arena in Provo, all while encountering fewer than half a dozen traffic lights and within two hours.

Such is the physical economy of the Salt Lake Games. In terms of convenience and ease of access, the 2002 Olympic Winter Games will be something of a throwback to the early days of the movement when all events were held in the same village.

The host city of Salt Lake is the focal point, with 10 venues that fan out from the city center all within a radius of 55 miles. From the Main Media Center in the heart of the city, no venue will be much more than an hour's drive away. Most will be considerably closer.

The venues could have been even more compact, with all facilities for the indoor competitions built within the boundaries of Salt Lake City itself and all the skiing, boarding and sliding events held in the mountains immediately east of the city. But organizers envisioned an Olympic Winter Games that would embrace the whole of the greater Salt Lake metropolitan area, and the planners set up the venues accordingly.

Not only will Salt Lake City participate in the 2002 Games, so will its neighbors. The areas of action have been expanded 50 miles to the Ogden area in the north, 50 miles to the Provo area in the south, 10 miles to West Valley City in the west, 15 miles to Kearns in the southwest and 50 miles to Park City and the Heber Valley in the east. The result is an Olympic circle that incorporates the length and

LOOKING WEST OVER THE CITY,
WITH THE GREAT SALT LAKE IN
THE BACKGROUND

breadth of the Wasatch Front. This means that, in one way or another, the 2002 Games will touch all 1.5 million people who live along that perimeter.

It also means that, no matter what your vantage point, an Olympic venue or attraction will not be far away. If you stand in the center of Salt Lake City's historic downtown area, it will be difficult to turn around without bumping into one. One major venue, the figure skating rink, and four important ancillary areas, including the Olympic Stadium, the Olympic Village, the Main Media Center and the Olympic Medals Plaza, will be located at or near downtown.

Although all the venues of 2002 are in relatively close proximity to one another, each will be unique in the sports it serves and the personality of the surrounding area. And with the considerable differences in elevation—some of the skiing events will be near 11,000 feet while events on the valley floor will be closer to 4,000 feet—even the weather will be of considerable contrast from one venue to another.

Here's a closer look at each of the venues and other key Olympic areas that will make up the Salt Lake City Olympic map:

FACING EAST PAST TRIAD CENTER
TOWARD OLYMPIC MEDALS PLAZA

RICE-ECCLES OLYMPIC STADIUM

The Salt Lake 2002 Games will begin and end here, starting with the Opening Ceremony on Friday 8 February 2002 and finishing with the Closing Ceremony 17 days later on Sunday 24 February.

Located in the foothills east of downtown, the stadium has been in position on the campus of the University of Utah since 1927. Numerous expansions have taken place over the decades, the most recent an Olympic-inspired renovation concluded in 1995 that nearly doubled seating capacity from 35,000 to 56,000. Also, individual chair seats were installed throughout.

The stadium floor is covered with artificial turf, suitable for the weather expected at the 2002 Games. All seats have unobstructed views in the bowl-shaped arena, but at the Opening Ceremony, perhaps the best place to be will be halfway up in the west stands, with a generous view of the parade of nations below and a direct shot of the snow-covered Wasatch Mountains in the east. The imagery of the youth of the world about to challenge the mountains will be inescapable.

OLYMPIC MEDALS PLAZA

In a converted parking lot adjacent to both the Main Media Center and the Salt Lake Ice Center, the

victors will receive their spoils—and thousands will salute them in standing ovation.

Nightly medals ceremonies honoring each day's gold, silver and bronze medalists will be held at the eastern end of Olympic Medals Plaza, which covers the space of an entire city block and will be able to accommodate up to 30,000 spectators. Within easy walking distance of the plaza are all downtown hotels, restaurants, office buildings, parking lots and light-rail train stations.

Given its proximity to the Main Media Center, it stands to reason that the view from the Olympic Medals Plaza of downtown Salt Lake City and the mountains in the background will become the signature picture of the Games. Watch for this image to be broadcast and rebroadcast around the world nightly by TV cameras focusing on the medal winners and the magnificent, snow-tipped backdrop behind them.

OLYMPIC VILLAGE

In 1862, the United States Army laid the foundation for an encampment that would house and protect their troops on the east bench of Salt Lake City. Little did they realize that nearly a century and a half later, that same encampment would house and protect the

UNIVERSITY OF UTAH CAMPUS,
WITH OLYMPIC VILLAGE
IN FAR BACKGROUND

The University of Utah, founded in 1850, is the oldest public institution of higher learning west of the Mississippi River. Although all programs at the university have their strengths, and faculty members are recognized among the nation's most prolific researchers, the University of Utah Medical Center is the showcase. Here the first artificial kidney and heart were developed and transplanted. Forty-five miles to the south is Brigham Young University, the largest private church-owned university in the United States. BYU is nationally recognized for its strong undergraduate and graduate programs. The state's educational values are expressed in these and the many smaller colleges and universities in Utah's system of higher education.

athletes competing in the XIX Olympic Winter Games—with some modern upgrades, of course.

The Olympians who will gather in Salt Lake will find their temporary homes in the old parade grounds, commissaries and rifle ranges that once were part of the Army compound of Fort Douglas. Here construction began in 1994 on units that will house the 3,500 athletes and officials of 2002 as well as serve as student housing for the University of Utah.

A post office, dry cleaner, game room, gift shop, restaurant, bowling alley and, of course, a physical therapy and workout center will all be a part of the home-away-from-home Olympic Village. Some athletes and officials competing exclusively in nordic events at Soldier Hollow will stay in facilities closer to that venue.

MAIN MEDIA CENTER

In most past Games, there have been two locales for the media to do their work: the Main Press Center, or MPC, for the written media, and the International Broadcast Center, or IBC, for the electronic media.

In Salt Lake, however, both the written and electronic media will be under one roof. That massive roof covers a 430,000-square-foot convention hall

MAIN MEDIA CENTER

INSIDE THE MAIN MEDIA CENTER

known in non-Olympic times as the Salt Palace. The IBC will be situated on one end, the MPC on the other. In total, the facility will be known as the Main Media Center, or MMC.

The Salt Palace is one of America's largest civic and convention centers. Several major trade shows use the facility annually. For the 2002 Games, more than 9,000 accredited media members will set up headquarters here. During each of the 17 days of the Games, literally millions of words and thousands of miles of videotape will be dispersed throughout the world, all originating from the MMC.

Located in the heart of downtown, the MMC will be within easy reach from lodgings for a majority of the media, who will be staying nearby in a variety of hotels and apartment buildings. Direct bus service to all venues will leave directly from the MMC's front entrance.

SALT LAKE ICE CENTER

No stranger to big-time events, the Salt Lake Ice Center carves the heart out of an arena that serves as the permanent home of the National Basketball Association's Utah Jazz. The arena seats nearly 20,000 for NBA games but will play host to just

under 11,000 for figure skating and short track speed skating events.

In its spot next to the Main Media Center, the Olympic Medals Plaza, the downtown business district and the beginning terminal of the light-rail system, the Ice Center is the most strategically located of all Olympic venues.

THE ICE SHEET AT OGDEN

Adjacent to the campus of Weber State University on the south side of Ogden, The Ice Sheet will play host to the men's and women's curling tournaments. With a seating capacity of 2,000, this is the most intimate of the venues, affording good viewing of the curling action, which will at times feature simultaneous competition on both of the side-by-side courts. The Ice Sheet is 30 miles from downtown Salt Lake.

UTAH OLYMPIC OVAL

Fifteen miles west of Salt Lake, the Olympic Oval features the most unusual architecture of the Salt Lake venues. With a clear-span roof equal to the size of a football field, the structure suggests fluidity even when standing still. Appropriately, the 6,500-seat

CURLING WILL BE AN OLYMPIC MEDAL EVENT FOR THE FIRST TIME IN 2002

THE ICE SHEET, OGDEN, UTAH

Oval will be the site of all 10 speed skating races of the Olympic Winter Games.

E CENTER

The E Center, located just nine miles from the Main Media Center, will be the primary arena for men's hockey and will also feature some women's hockey games. With a seating capacity of 8,500, the arena is no stranger to hockey matches and hockey crowds. When it isn't hosting the Games, it is home to Salt Lake's International Hockey League entry, the Grizzlies.

THE PEAKS ICE ARENA

Fifty-five miles from downtown Salt Lake, The Peaks Ice Arena allows the citizens of Utah Valley to participate in the hosting of the Olympic Winter Games of 2002. Two full-size rinks reserved for Olympic usage beginning a full month before the start of the Games will afford valuable pre-Games ice time for hockey teams, figure skaters and others with ice needs. Once the 2002 Games are under way, The Peaks Ice Arena will be used for preliminary round men's hockey games and will be the primary venue for the women's hockey tournament.

E CENTER

In the wake of the Olympic Winter Games will be
the VIII Paralympic Winter Games, starting 7
March 2002. Nearly 1,100 athletes and officials
from 35 nations will participate in 35 medal events.
Ice sledge, shown opposite, is a popular event that
will be hosted in the E Center.

SNOWBASIN SKI AREA

Tucked into the back side of massive Mount Ogden, the Snowbasin Ski Area, Utah's third-oldest winter resort, will be the site of downhill, downhill combined and Super-G alpine ski racing.

The downhill courses were designed by noted Swiss downhiller Bernhard Russi, a gold medalist in that event in Sapporo in 1972. Russi also designed the Olympic downhill courses used in Albertville in 1992 and Nagano in 1998. When the downhill architect first laid eyes on the steep and challenging terrain at Snowbasin, he proclaimed it a "gift from God."

PARK CITY MOUNTAIN RESORT

Snowboard and giant slalom alpine ski racers will compete on courses sitting literally atop thousands of miles of mine tunnels. Those tunnels were once at the heart of the principal activity in this resort that lies adjacent to the century-old mining town of Park City.

The Park City Mountain Resort has the most world-class experience of any of the 2002 venues. Dating back to 1986, it has played host to numerous men's and women's alpine skiing World Cup events over the years, and the city houses the headquarters

PARK CITY SKI RUNS

for numerous winter sports organizations, including the United States Ski and Snowboard Association.

DEER VALLEY RESORT

Freestyle aerials and moguls competition will take place at this ski resort, which neighbors the Park City Mountain Resort. Men's and women's alpine slalom skiers will also compete here. Located 35 miles from downtown Salt Lake City, both Deer Valley and Park City Mountain Resort are accessible by freeway and major four-lane highways. The combined spectator capacity of the two resorts will be nearly 40,000, making the greater Park City area—with its numerous shops, restaurants and ski runs—a prime gathering point of the Games.

SOLDIER HOLLOW

Busiest of all the venues will be this cross-country skiing layout situated in the rolling foothills of Wasatch Mountain State Park on the eastern slope of the Wasatch Range. At a minimum altitude of 1,670 meters (about 5,000 feet) and a maximum altitude of 1,793 meters (about 5,500 feet), a variety of courses will test athletes competing in cross-country skiing, biathlon and nordic combined events. In all, 23

CROSS-COUNTRY SKIER AT OLYMPIC TEST EVENT, SOLDIER HOLLOW

events will be contested at Soldier Hollow during a scheduled 16 straight days of competition.

Situated just around the corner from Deer Creek Reservoir and at the apron of towering Mount Timpanogos in the distance, Soldier Hollow will feature a stadium with a 20,000-spectator capacity.

UTAH OLYMPIC PARK

Located 25 miles east of Salt Lake City and 5 miles north of Park City, the Utah Olympic Park comprises the bobsled, luge and skeleton track and the K90 and K120 ski jumps. By the time of the 2002 Games, several world-class events will have been held to test both the sliding track and the jumps.

By building this venue, local Olympic planners first signaled to the USOC and the IOC how determined Salt Lake was to get the Games. When construction began in the spring of 1991, Salt Lake had no guarantees that these facilities—only the second of their kind in the United States—would ever be put to Olympic use. At 9:00 in the morning on Saturday 9 February 2002, when the first Olympic competitor receives the signal to ski down the ramp and jump off the K90 hill on the first day of competition, the gamble will have paid off with a thrilling reality.

A BOBSLED RACES DOWN THE TRACK AT THE UTAH OLYMPIC PARK

THOUGH NOT AN OFFICIAL venue, the spirit of the
Olympic Winter Games will fill in all the gaps and
crevices of the 2002 Games, permeating the whole of
the Olympic corridor as it has done for more than a
century during the modern era. It is this spirit that
always brings to life a variety of events and extrava-
ganzas whenever an Olympic Games makes an
appearance. Salt Lake City will be no exception, with
plans under way on many fronts for cultural, artistic
and social experiences, all with an Olympic flavor.
Among these events will be the "Lure of the West:
Treasures from the Smithsonian's American Art
Museum" art show at Brigham Young University, the
"Quilts Across America" exhibit at the Salt Lake
City International Airport courtesy of the American
Craft Museum, and performances by the Utah
Symphony, Ballet West and other theatrical compa-
nies housed along the Wasatch Front.

   Pin trading, ice sculpting, face painting, flag
waving, street dancing—all will be a part of the
Olympic experience, turning the mountains and val-
leys of the Wasatch Front into a place that, for
17 days of glory, will be one of truly Olympic
proportions.

We gratefully acknowledge KODAK PROFESSIONAL
for their film sponsorship. All photographs made
specifically for this project were made using
Kodak Professional Ektachrome E100VS.